LOG CABINS *of* ALASKA

PHOTOGRAPHY AND STORIES BY HARRY M. WALKER

To Sally . . . with love.

Project Editor: Kent Sturgis
Text Editors: Christine Ummel and Victoria Sturgis
Cover and Book Design: Elizabeth Watson
Proofreader: Lois Kelly
Printer: C&C Offset Printing Co., Ltd.
Production Manager: Kent Sturgis

Front cover: Kerosene lamps and hanging flower baskets decorate the eaves of a family cabin in Tok (center); Christmas lights adorn a pioneer couple's cabin in Anchorage (upper left); a log cache with moose rack attached combine two Alaskan icons in Anchorage (upper right); a sagging barn in the Matanuska valley (lower right); a husky snoozes atop his log doghouse at Denali National Park (lower left). Page 1: Bright, colorful flowers contrast the weathered logs of a cabin near Dyea in Southeast Alaska.

To order single copies of LOG CABINS OF ALASKA, mail $14.95 each (Washington residents add $1.20 sales tax) plus $3 for shipping to: Epicenter Press, Box 82368, Kenmore, WA 98028.

Booksellers: This book is available from major wholesalers. Retail discounts are available from our trade distributor, Graphic Arts Center Publishing Company, Box 10306, Portland, OR 97210. Phone 800-452-3032.

PRINTED IN HONG KONG

First Printing, May 1999

10 9 8 7 6 5 4 3 2 1

▶ A log cabin ice cream shop in Wasilla.

FOREWORD

Harry Walker's wonderful pictures and stories of Alaska's ruggedly diverse log cabins and the strong-willed, independent people who craft them by hand and live and work in them could have been titled "America's Log Home Dream Book." These Alaskans are living a fantasy shared by many Americans. Far from this last frontier, many can only imagine life in a log home. Yet their dreams are as rich and textured as the stories here. Many of us first discovered the warmth of logs at summer camps, ski lodges, parks, and historic places. These log buildings may have been rustic and appealingly simple, nostalgic reminders of an earlier time when life was slower and less complicated. Today, log home living is alive and well from coast to coast in the Lower 48—in New England, throughout the Appalachians, along the Great Lakes, and of course in the West. For some, the appeal is as simple as a decorating style, a showcase for an antique collection. For other more ambitious folks, it represents a chance to live their lives differently, off the beaten path as chosen by the new breed of pioneers chronicled in this book. People fall in love with the charm of log homes and think, "I could build a home with my own hands." And they can. They do. As these stories prove.

Janice Brewster, Editor
Log Home Living magazine

CONTENTS

33 An icon of life in Alaska, the log cache is part family attic, part winter freezer.

20 One down and lots more to go in Phil Zastrow's single-handed attempt to build an entire town of log buildings.

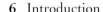

24 The Reverend Bert Bingle named it The Church of a Thousand Trees, but who's counting?

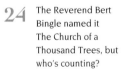

34 Kevin Foster loves Victorian architecture but learned that incorporating it into a log home was easier said than done.

4

INTRODUCTION

There is no more enduring symbol of the American pioneering spirit than the log cabin. These structures recall for us a time lost to modern society. Whether or not such a time ever really existed—a time of self-reliance, courage, honesty, and simplicity—America's longing for it has been exploited by advertisers and politicians for nearly two hundred years. Presidents Jackson, Buchanan, Polk, and Garfield were all born in log cabins and often used their origins to their political advantage. And even honest old Abe Lincoln was known to make the most of his humble

log cabin beginnings. Never mind that the log cabin was a Scandinavian import. Log cabins have become a symbol in America of a time gone by. Little wonder then that they should be so closely associated with a place called "The Last Frontier." From Emmonak to Eagle, Ketchikan to Koyukuk, Sutton to Sitka, log buildings are a common feature of the Alaska landscape. Many are old, dating to the Russian colonial period or to one of the great Alaska gold rushes. Most of them were built for the same reasons that log cabins went up across the Great Plains and the West during the western expansion: people needed immediate shelter made from readily available materials. Alaska's history, however, is still remarkably, well . . . recent. Unlike America's earlier frontiers, where few original log structures remain, Alaska's log buildings haven't been around long enough to fully suffer the ravages of time and progress. Miners' cabins of the late nineteenth century, though poorly constructed, dot the landscape. And log buildings from the Russian Colonial period (many of them churches) have survived as well, mostly hidden under clapboard siding. Log cabins in Alaska are not just historical oddities. Alaskans live, work, play, and pray in their log buildings. And while in the rest of the United States modern log cabins come in kits that are assembled like a giant set of Lincoln Logs®, Alaska has the real thing: log buildings built by hand with local materials. The truth is log cabins are still practical in the North. 🏠 Yet it is more than the practical, more than the pioneering spirit that draws Alaskans to logs. Logs provide a connection to the natural world otherwise missing in a house constructed with

modern materials. Vinyl siding and roof shingles may make our lives easier, but they also make our homes increasingly artificial. The visceral pleasure of living surrounded by logs is not unlike the pleasure derived from walking barefoot on a beach, driving along an interstate in a convertible with the top down, or simply breathing air thick with the smell of lilacs. It's hard to imagine anyone getting that much pleasure from living in a house of Sheetrock® and plastic laminate. 🏠 The special bond that develops between cabin dweller and cabin may seem a little naive, perhaps even a little hokey to the rest of us. But listen to these people talk about their log cabins and you will know that for them the connection is very real and personal.

◀◀ Log cabin rentals built all in a row in Fairbanks.
◀ A hunter's fly-in cabin deep in the Alaska Range.
▲ A cabin on the lower Yukon River has seen its better days.

LOG-ICAL CHOICE

▲ The Blue Berry Lodge has been open for business since 1991.
▶ The warm and comfortable interior is a haven in Juneau's rainy climate.

After talking with Jay and Judy Urquhart for a few minutes, it is easy to see that they make quite a team. ▤ "When we were ready to build the Blue Berry Lodge, we considered every type of construction known," Jay said in the dining room of their four-thousand square-foot Juneau bed-and-breakfast. ▤ "We looked at underground structures, domes, post and beam, and even something called Solarcrete® [foam core and sprayed concrete]," added Judy. ▤ "We settled with log. It had warmth, coziness, lots of appeal, always a rich feel," Jay continued. These characteristics are indeed important in a town that receives more than sixty inches of rain annually. ▤ "It felt fifty years old the day it was done," Judy said. Jay nodded in agreement. ▤ According to Jay, Judy designed

the building. "We used to drive down the road and Judy would knock on doors to ask about the houses." She took features from here and there to come up with the ideal space. Though he didn't harvest the logs himself, Jay did almost everything else, constructing the lodge while working full-time as a hard-rock miner. "I was working on about three hours of sleep a night for a year." Since the lodge opened in 1991, Jay and Judy have had all sorts of guests, from presidential advisors to professional athletes. They have hosted weddings and held retreats. Many visitors come back again and again. Jay and Judy think people choose the Blue Berry Lodge because it's a log structure. Well, that may explain why people visit the first time, but the warmth and charm of Judy and Jay Urquhart is no doubt why they return.

▲ A temperate rain forest surrounds the Blue Berry Lodge.
◀ ▲ The lodge's solid comfort brings guests back again and again.

HOME IN THE RANGE

▲ An Iditarod athlete takes a break during the race to Nome.
▶ Rohn Roadhouse is a favorite checkpoint on the Iditarod Trail.

For a handful of days each winter, the old Bureau of Land Management cabin at Rohn, built in 1929, serves as a checkpoint along the 1,100-mile route of the Iditarod Trail Sled Dog Race between Anchorage and Nome. Fifty mushers, a dozen or so race officials, several media people, and more than six hundred dogs use the fourteen-by-twenty-foot cabin as a combination restaurant, hotel, veterinary clinic, workshop, and communications facility. ▦ There are two dozen checkpoints along the Iditarod Trail—remote lodges, temporary shelters, private cabins, villages—but nothing quite like Rohn. Perhaps it's the spectacular scenery of the Alaska Range. Perhaps the mushers are just happy to have

made it there after the long climb through Rainy Pass and the sometimes terrifying descent through the Dalzell Gorge. Whatever the reason, folks talk about the Rohn cabin in words normally reserved for old lovers. "You should have seen her last year before they put on the new door and windows," one race official said as we stood outside, waiting for the next dog team to arrive. "She was beautiful." He took a moment, looked over at the cabin, a gentle look crossing his unshaven face. "She's sure a snug, sweet little thing."

▲ Mushers pause for coffee, conversation, and perhaps a little sleep.
◀ A snow-clad peak and a frozen lake in the Alaska Range.

CECIL'S PUZZLE

In 1937 Cecil Rhode built an eighteen-by-twenty-three-foot log cabin on three acres along the shore of Kenai Lake near Cooper Landing, a tiny community on the Kenai Peninsula. Cecil thought the cabin so spacious that he included a darkroom, perhaps one of the first log cabin darkrooms in Alaska. ▦ When Cecil returned to Alaska from Seattle just after World War II, he returned a married man, and his spacious log cabin no longer seemed so spacious. Cecil's darkroom was the first thing to go, converted into a closet for his new wife, Helen. In 1957 their son David was born and the cabin seemed

▲ An outdoor bathtub with a spectacular view of Kenai Lake.
▶ The bigger and better log cabin Cecil Rhode built for his family in 1962.

smaller still. Helen's closet became David's bedroom. 🏠 By 1962 Cecil had had enough. The family needed a larger cabin. They decided to move the cabin and live in it while Cecil built their new cabin on the original site. It may be common in some places to move a house to a new location, but moving a log cabin uphill across heavily wooded ground in Alaska is altogether different. 🏠 Undeterred, Cecil cleared a few trees and built a big slide with a winch. "Cecil took the cabin apart log by log," David told me. "He numbered the logs, cupboards, shelves . . . everything was put back together just the way it was. Cecil was a watchmaker as a boy, and he had a great sense of precision."

◄ ▲ The interior of Cecil's original bachelor log cabin built in 1937.
▲ Cecil moved the original cabin board by board and log by log to this spot before beginning work on the new one.

FUNKY CHICKEN

The story goes something like this: Gold miners working claims in the heart of the Fortymile Mining District east of Fairbanks decided to name their growing settlement "Ptarmigan." Unfortunately, no one there was certain how to spell the word, and since miners had long referred to the common bird as a "wild chicken," the name "Chicken" was substituted. 🏛 Robin Hammond has lived with the consequences of that decision since she became the town postmaster in 1992. You see, Chicken, Alaska, with a little help

▲ Looking for chicken memorabilia? Visit the Post Office in Chicken.
▶ Postmaster Robin Hammond on the front porch of a government-issue log cabin post office.

▲ Robin keeps in touch with neighbors via CB radio.
▶ ▲ A gold dredge decays alongside the Taylor Highway.

from Robin, has become the Graceland for chicken lovers. "People send letters and cards all the time, asking for a postmark. I stamp it officially and then I add some rubber chicken stamps I have collected over the years," Robin said from inside the tiny log post office. 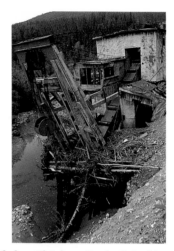 "There is a woman from Eau Claire, Wisconsin, who calls herself the Chicken Lady," Robin continued. "She wrote last year and said she was coming to Chicken for a visit. She showed up with chicken everything: chicken earrings, chicken shoes, chicken shirt, and chicken hat. I started showing her some of the stuff I have, and she said, 'I have found my bosom buddy!' We have been swapping chicken gifts ever since." Robin's own collection of chicken paraphernalia is extensive. There's chicken wallpaper, chicken wall hangings, chicken paintings, chicken bric-a-brac, and of course a rubber chicken. "I have lots of stuff, but I'm too chicken to put it up," Robin said with a perfectly straight face.

15

CUTTING CORNERS

Anyone who is not a log cabin aficionado may have trouble understanding all the fuss over the way log walls are put together. But log joinery can say a lot about the skill, patience level, and amount of time available to a craftsman. 🏠 The simplest joinery is the lap joint, though to purists (and there are lots of them) "the butt and run" joint, as it is also called, isn't a real joint at all because the rounds are alternately lapped and spiked together. A purist will tell you that locking logs together without spikes or nails is the only way to make a real log joint. 🏠 Many craftsmen prefer the round notch,

▲ A red squirrel examines the end of a round notch joint.
▶ An old example of a saddle-notch joint.
▶ ▶ A "butt and run" or simple lap joint.

constructed by cutting a round notch in the underside of a log so that it locks over the top of the log beneath it in the adjoining wall, just like Lincoln Logs®. While not perfect, this joint is strong, nail-free, and less susceptible to rot. 🏚 Other joints also have their devotees and critics. There's the V-notch, saddle notch, half and full dovetail notch, spline notch, flat or square notch joints, as well as tenon notch joints with or without corner posts. There are nearly as many log joints as there are craftsmen to make them.

◀ ◀ A full dovetail joint in Nenana.
◀ A log-smith's favorite: the round notch joint.

CIVIC-MINDED CITY

For eighty-four years, the entire city government of Eagle, Alaska, fit into a seventeen-by-nineteen-foot log cabin built in 1901. When the city budget is $68,000 and only $4,000 in property tax is collected each year, government doesn't need a lot of space. Then in 1985 a $30,000 log addition was built behind the original cabin, nearly doubling the space. Now records are stored in the old city hall along with the city's lone voting booth,

▲ The double-door entrance to Eagle's original city hall, built in 1901.
▶ For eighty-four years, this tiny cabin housed Eagle's city government.

while all other business, including city council meetings, is conducted in the new space. When I asked city mayor Jerry Nelson how many residents regularly attend council meetings, he answered, "Usually just my wife." 🏛 There was a time, however, when Eagle's population was a lot more civic-minded. Of course, that was in 1959, when the town had only nine residents and seven of them were on the city council.

▲ Eagle's only voting booth inside the original log cabin.
◀ In 1985, a log addition enlarged the Eagle City Hall.

ONE MAN'S MAIN STREET

When Phil Zastrow observed that the great old-fashioned "Main Streets" had all but disappeared in Alaska, he decided to build his own in North Pole. "My Main Street will have about twenty stores, a couple of gift shops, a church, some rental cabins, and a drive-through espresso stand with a large wooden version of the starship *Enterprise* mounted on the roof, all of it made of logs," Phil said as he worked on the second story of a commissioned cabin. 🏠 While the thought of building an entire town out of logs might

▲ Phil Zastrow with daughter Joesi.
▶ Phil works on the second story of a commissioned log cabin in North Pole.

be daunting to most, it isn't to Phil. "I figure it will take me seven years," he said. To generate some revenue for the rest of the project, he plans to build the rental cabins and espresso stand first. Phil already has a sawmill set up on his twelve-acre site near North Pole, and a year-round state logging permit to clear twenty acres of timber near Delta Junction, a hundred miles away. What about the skills necessary to build an interstellar spaceship out of logs? "I taught myself how to work with logs," Phil told me. "Over the years I've made lots of mistakes, but now I can do almost anything with them." All Phil needs now is some free time. He receives commissions on all sorts of projects, from building cabins to carving eagle sculptures. When you have a wife and child to support, it's hard to turn down the work—even if there's a whole town just waiting to be built.

◄ ▲ Phil pauses to examine his work.
◄ ◄ One of the log cabins built by Phil for his one-man Main Street.
◄ Chips fly from Phil's hands-on approach.

COLONIAL CALAMITY

▲ An old piece of farm machinery on a Palmer field.
▶ One of the original pioneer log barns built in the Matanuska Valley Colony in 1937.
▶ ▶ Pioneer Peak forms a spectacular backdrop to a colony barn.

In the midst of the Great Depression, the federal government set out to do something it had never done before—establish a colony on its territory. In 1934, 202 families, over one thousand people in all, were brought by boat from San Francisco to Seward, Alaska, then by train to Palmer to establish the Matanuska Valley Colony. The government promised each family a forty-acre tract, a house, a barn, approximately $3,500 worth of credit toward supplies and machinery, and thirty years to repay their debt. On paper it seemed like a pretty good deal. Yet things got off to a shaky start. 🏠 Regardless of the skills the colonists had to offer, they were ordered to sit through the short Alaska summer while transient workers built the colony's houses and barns using plans developed in Washington, D.C. It didn't take long for them to see that a barn designed by folks with little or no experience in Alaska wasn't a very good idea, yet absolutely no deviations from the plans were permitted. So the colonists watched while strangers built barns for them on

untreated pilings that were quick to rot, that were drafty in the windy valley, and that at thirty-two square feet were too small to provide shelter to all the farm animals during the coldest months. 🏠 Little wonder that within four years sixty percent of the original colonists had abandoned their land . . . or perhaps, more amazing that forty percent stayed on.

THE CHURCH OF "HOW MANY TREES?"

▲ Tim Carrick, pastor of the all-log United Protestant Church in Palmer. ▶ and ▶ ▶ A decorative mix of horizontal and vertical logs was used in the construction of the "Church of a Thousand Trees."

While the federal government was trying to establish a colony in the Matanuska Valley, the Presbyterian Church of the United States sent the Reverend Bert Bingle to build a church there. By early 1936, after a stint in a wall tent, Rev. Bingle decided to build a more permanent structure and turned to the federal government for materials. For fifty dollars he acquired a permit which entitled him to harvest a thousand trees. According to church records, only 996 trees were used. ▤ Somehow "the Church of Nine Hundred and Ninety-Six Trees" didn't sound very inspirational, so when it was time for the Palmer church to be officially dedicated on April 11, 1937, the Reverend Bingle was installed

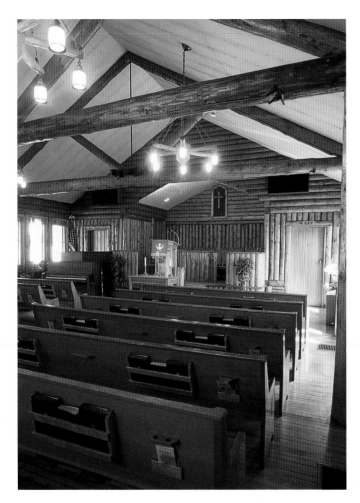

as the first pastor of "the Church of a Thousand Trees." Over the years, additions to the building have probably increased the number of logs to well over a thousand, but no one knows for sure. Even Tim Carrick, church pastor at the United Protestant Church since 1991, admits to having doubts. "I've thought about counting the logs myself," he told me. "But the way they have been cut up, I wouldn't know where one log ends and another starts."

▲ The Reverend Bert Bingle replaced a canvas wall tent with this log church in 1937.

BLONDIE'S BUNNY BOOKS

▲ A plaster statue of Blondie, a white German Shepherd companion of Daniel Frederick's prior to her death.
▶ Blondie's Antiques operates in downtown Fairbanks from a log cabin built in 1905.

There's the handwritten thesis from 1729, the 1870s wooden sleigh, the 1930s Mickey Mouse® statue, the working 1954 Seeburg® jukebox, and much, much more in the 1906 log cabin that houses Blondie's Antiques in Fairbanks. Owner Daniel Frederick admits, "There are corners of this store I haven't seen in ten years." 🏛 Daniel decided to go into business for himself in 1984, just after closure of the local Army-Navy store he managed, He moved the store's inventory of Alaska's favorite winter boots, nicknamed "bunny boots," into the cabin and began gathering antiques on his travels. Simultaneously he

opened Blondie's Goldmine in the basement of the cabin, offering tourists an opportunity to pan for gold and view his mining memorabilia. Three years later his life turned a little upside down. "They were going to kill this wonderful thirty-two-year-old horse named Misty," Daniel explained. "I couldn't let them do it." Daniel converted the store into a stable, suspended operations in Blondie's Goldmine, and moved himself downstairs. Misty survived a year. After that Daniel concentrated on selling antiques. He admitted that selling antiques to tourists is a tough sell. "Tour guides always point out the place as they go by. When tourists stop they like to look but they don't buy." And who's Blondie? "I have had several Blondies over the years. This one," Daniel said, pointing to a huge

white German Shepherd filling nearly all the empty space by the front door, "this one is called Prince Charming. He's the male version."

◄◄ "There are corners of this store I haven't seen in ten years," said Daniel Frederick.
◄ A male version of Blondie, Prince Charming, peers out the shop's front window.

CHIP OFF THE OLD BLOCK

In 1799, Aleksandr Andreevich Baranov of the Russian America Company ordered a log fortification built on a promontory on the western shore of what is now called Baranof Island. After local Tlingit Indians burned it down in 1802, Baranov had it rebuilt in 1804. From 1808 until the sale of Alaska to the United States in 1867, that log fort, which evolved into the town of Sitka, was the center of government, religion, trade, and culture in Russian America. Over the years, scores of Russian-style log buildings were built within its walls—lavish houses for government and religious officials, barracks for Russian and Aleut employees, storage sheds for otter pelts, and even a large Russian Orthodox Church—it was a virtual log metropolis. Yet by the middle of this century

▲ This replica of a Russian Blockhouse was built in 1962 on the site of the original stockade.
▶ An example of nineteenth-century Russian architecture in Sitka.

▲ The blockhouse uses hewn logs with double lapped joints.
◄ A vista of fishing boats and mountain peaks is easy on the eyes in Sitka.

the stockade and nearly all of the Russian log buildings were gone and the few remaining were covered by siding or otherwise altered beyond recognition. In 1962 the National Park Service decided to restore a bit of Russian log architecture to Sitka and built a replica of one of the four log blockhouses that were originally attached to the stockade wall. And what once might have seemed quite commonplace sitting in the center of town, now seems about as out-of-place as a grain silo in the middle of New York City.

ANOTHER CHINK IN THE WALL

▲ Lorna McDermott stands in the doorway of her cabin in Dyea.
▶ John and Lorna McDermott bought the old cabin in 1976.

Chinking a cabin—that is, filling the air spaces between rounds of logs—is one of the most time-consuming and least-fun parts of cabin construction. 🏠 "When we bought the place in 1976," John McDermott told me, while standing outside the small cabin he shares with his wife Lorna along the Taiya River in Dyea, "someone had chinked the logs with felt and covered it with willow strips. It looked nice but the felt absorbed water and started to rot the logs. We had to pull it all out. We tried various materials after that, including a cement mix." 🏠 John and his wife left Dyea in 1982, shortly after the White Pass and Yukon Route Railroad closed in nearby Skagway, leaving John without a job. They returned in 1993, after the trains started operating again. 🏠 "We got back in the

dead of winter," John said, "We discovered that all of the chinking had opened up. That first night we could have flown a kite upstairs." 🏠 The next morning John drove the eight miles to Skagway and bought every can of spray polyurethane insulating foam that Skagway Hardware had in stock. "The problem with the foam is you can't use it in the cold," John explained. "I spent the day heating the stuff up on the stove just enough so it wouldn't explode. Then I would run outside, spray the stuff 'til the can froze up, come back in, and start over again."

◄▲ John "chinked" the drafty cabin with spray insulating foam.
▲▲ The Dyea Valley is their backyard.
▲ The McDermott cabin blends naturally with its surroundings.

CABIN INCOGNITO

▲ An onion dome with cross rises above an octagonal belfry on the Holy Assumption Russian Orthodox Church in Kenai.

Some of the most beautiful, most photographed, and most un-log-like looking buildings in Alaska are Russian Orthodox Churches. So you can imagine my surprise when I discovered that hidden under the attractive white clapboard siding on many of them is a log cabin! Well, perhaps not a log cabin exactly; a building containing a narthex, a nave and a sanctuary is hardly a log cabin. 🏠 Why the disguise? At first I was sure it was all a matter of aesthetics. Log cabin pioneers on the American frontier couldn't wait to get into more aesthetically pleasing European-style houses. But Russian log church buildings were covered with siding to improve their energy efficiency, not just their looks. Seems that walls made from rough-hewn logs (as all these churches were) and covered with clapboard siding are thicker and tighter, therefore less susceptible to air filtration than are walls made with traditional round logs. 🏠 I can relate. Once many years ago I lived in a cabin where the walls were so thin and so poorly insulated I had to put stuff in my refrigerator at night (yes, I did have electricity) just to keep it from freezing.

◄ Clapboard siding applied over a surface of hewn logs improves the building's energy efficiency

CACHING IN

People from outside Alaska may think of the igloo as the ultimate in Alaska architecture, but the true icon of life in Alaska is the log cache: part winter freezer, part animal-proof warehouse, part family attic. 🏠 For untold generations, Native peoples of Alaska have used elevated storehouses. Little wonder that as the tide of miners and trappers swept across Alaska in the late nineteenth century, they saw the practicality of a cache and appropriated it for their own use. Pictures and descriptions of caches appeared in books, newspapers, magazines, paintings, and poems around the world. Before long, Alaska's romantic, pioneering image came to include a log cache sitting next to a log cabin. 🏠 Today, when a local business wants to communicate to Alaskans, "Hey, we're one of you," a log cache is the perfect vehicle. It comes in all shapes and sizes, in front of all sorts of businesses—from a box the size of a loaf of bread raised about a foot off the ground to a garage-size building on stilts tall enough to weather The Great Flood.

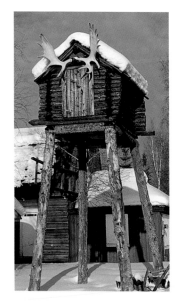

▲ A "typical" log cache in Alaskaland, a park built in Fairbanks for the centennial celebration of Alaska's purchase from Russia.
▶▶ and ▶ When business owners search for the perfect symbol that says "Alaska," many choose the log cache.

A TOWERING ACHIEVEMENT

▲ Tess Riley peers out from her favorite treehouse.
▶ Peggy Foster with her children, Tess and Riley, in the lower level of their two-story log turret.

When Peggy and Kevin Foster moved onto their property about six miles outside of Talkeetna in 1984, the twenty-by-twenty-four-foot cabin was already there and in rough shape. "It was bad," said Peggy. "We redid it: jacked it up off the ground, put in a ceiling, put in a well. We did everything." The arrival of their first child in 1990 triggered a period of expansion that more than doubled the cabin size and gave it a distinct look. "I've always loved the Victorian style," Kevin explained. "I wanted to see if I could do it with logs." Peggy and Kevin differ on how long it took to build the addition and

two-storey turret. "It took about eight months to finish," Kevin said. "I think it actually took almost two years," Peggy corrected. Except for the logs themselves, everything else had to be brought in by snow machine or all-terrain vehicle. "We dragged the couch in on a sled behind the snow machine," Kevin told me. And is all the effort that goes into living in the bush worth it? "After we were out here a year or two we spent a week in Talkeetna [population 256] house-sitting for a friend and it was horrid," Peggy said. "So much noise and activity. We couldn't wait to come home."

▲ A bountiful flower garden celebrates the summer season.
◀ "I've always loved the Victorian style," said Kevin Foster.

A HOPE-FUL OCCASION

"Hope is my spiritual center," David McCabe explained, describing his wedding in 1997 to Rebecca Harper in a little town called Hope on the Kenai Peninsula. "It's been my family's summer place since I was four. . . . It's a powerful place. Rebecca's parents [from San Jose, California] were a little dubious, but once they got there they appreciated why." 🏠 "We actually thought about having the wedding at the family cabin," Rebecca said, "but David's family said it wouldn't work. We looked at the Methodist Church, but it was too small." Rebecca couldn't remember exactly how they decided on the social hall. "I think it worked out pretty well, though," she continued. "It looked cool and only cost

▲ and ▶ Guests gather around the log cabin social hall for David and Rebecca's wedding reception.

ten dollars to rent." To free up space inside for dancing, David and Rebecca arranged for a couple of tents to be set up next to the social hall for the reception. ⌂ According to Diane Olthuis, a long-time resident and member of the local historical society, the hall has been the center of Hope's social life for nearly one hundred years. "Since 1902," she said, "the hall has been used for miners' meetings, civic meetings, kid shows, talent shows, weddings, and lots of dances. In fact, it is famous for its dances, which were held almost every weekend back in the '30s. People came from as far away as Seward [nearly 75 miles]

for the dances." ⌂ "You know, there's just one thing I've noticed about the social hall over the years," Diane told me. "It seems to have shrunk as I've gotten older. It seemed so much bigger when I was young."

◄◄ "It looked cool and only cost ten dollars," said Rebecca about the Hope Social Hall.
◄ Tern Lake on the Kenai Peninsula.

LOG CABIN CUSTOMS

▲ U.S. customs officer Michael Thompson outside Poker Creek border station on the Top of the World Highway.
▶ Michael talks to the driver of a motor home seeking to enter Alaska from the Yukon Territory, Canada.

Each day it is Michael Thompson's job to open and close a country. As a U.S. customs officer, Michael moves a barrier across the Top of the World Highway at the Poker Creek border station. ⬛ The highway, which connects Dawson City, Yukon Territory, Canada with the Taylor Highway in Alaska, is open only twelve hours a day from mid-May through mid-September, weather permitting. "There isn't enough traffic to warrant keeping the road open twenty-four hours," Michael told me. "There are times when hardly a vehicle goes by all day and once the snow starts in September, forget it." ⬛ Records show that the customs log cabin has been at Poker Creek—or at least what everyone calls

Poker Creek—since 1977. Immigration officer Paul Kelly explained, "The station is actually located on Davis Creek, but they thought everyone would ask, 'Who is Davis?' and no one really knew." Paul shrugged. "We're close enough to Poker Creek, and that sounds more romantic anyway." 🏠 But now officials are talking about building a joint facility with Canada Customs, presently located in an RV trailer across the road, and tearing the log cabins down. That upsets both Michael and Paul. As Paul said, "If you think about Alaska, you think about log cabins. They belong here. I would hate to see them come down."

▲ A monument marks the border between the U.S. and Canada.
◄ "There are times when hardly a vehicle goes by all day," Michael Thompson said.

LIGHT SNACKS

Anchorage was a frontier city of fourteen thousand, covering just two square miles, when Ralph and Maxine Linsacum moved there from Wyoming in 1947 to build a twenty-by-thirty-foot cabin a couple of miles outside the city limits.  "It was fun for us to go to town then," Maxine told me, smiling. "Matanuska Maid had an ice cream store downtown. We would sit on a bench out front and just look at people going by." Ralph, sitting with us in the living room, remembered it took about two years to get electricity all the way out to their cabin, and neither could remember when they got their first phone.

▲ Ralph and Maxine Linsacum sit in the living room of their Anchorage log cabin.
▶ Christmas lights have adorned the Linsacum home every year since 1953.

After they built an addition to the original cabin in 1953, Ralph started putting up the Christmas lights. "The red star went up first," said Ralph. "People thought we were from Texas." He grinned. Ralph and Maxine added to the light display every year, and every year they struggled to keep moose from eating the lights. "They must really like the taste of those bulbs," Maxine said. Anchorage has changed over the years. Today the municipality covers almost seventeen hundred square miles, with a population over 260,000. Yet a few things remain the same. Ralph continues to put up the Christmas lights every year, with a little help from his grandson. And despite how much the city has grown around them, it's still a struggle to protect the lights from hungry moose.

◄ ◄ The moon peeks from behind the Chugach Mountains in Anchorage.
◄ Every year hungry moose snack on Ralph's light display.

41

DOGGIE DIGS

▲ A winter wonderland beckons visitors along the Parks Highway.
▶ A plaster sled dog sits atop a log kennel awaiting donations in Denali National Park.

Dog teams have been used for winter transportation in Denali National Park since the 1920s. With motor vehicles prohibited in a park the size of Massachusetts, sled dogs are the most practical way of conducting regular patrols. Although the dogs work hard all winter, they take the summer off, loafing around and greeting park visitors at the dog kennels, located behind park headquarters. ⌂ At most kennels in Alaska the individual doghouses are made from plywood, but in Denali they are made of logs. "The tourists love them," said Lori Yanuchi, a long-time musher and dog handler, as we stood in the middle of the dog yard. "Tourists ask

if they can get the plans to build them." 🏠 "Despite their looks, though, the kennels aren't as functional as you might think," she continued. "They are a little too big even for the dogs. We have to fill them with straw in the winter to keep the dogs warm."

▲ National Park Service musher and dog handler Lori Yanuchi visits with Shadow a four-month-old Alaska husky.
◄ Sled dog Sepp'la snoozes away a summer day on top of his personal residence.

BLAZING
THE WAY

Years before recycling swept the Lower 48, cabin dwellers in Alaska were confirmed believers. When you live hundreds of miles from the nearest home improvement center, you tend to hang on to things, lots of things, certain that sooner or later you will find a purpose for them. One of the things cabin dwellers hung onto were the five-gallon Chevron Blazo® cans that contained the fuel (white gas) which for years powered most appliances in the bush. Stacks of these cans piled up everywhere. ⌂ We may never know the name of that first cabin dweller who looked at his stash of empty Blazo® cans, then at the roof of his log cabin, and put the two together. We may never know if the first Blazo® can roof appeared in the town of Wiseman. Regardless, I think it is fair to say that in Wiseman the Blazo® can roof has reached its full architectural potential.

▲ Recycled fuel cans wait to be flattened into service as roof shingles.
▶ A Blazo® can roof adorns this compact one-man log cabin at Wiseman.

GROWING PAINS

"We've had a real bad year," Shawna Russell told me, excusing herself from behind the information desk at the log cabin visitor center in North Pole. She headed toward the back door and her garden hose, adding, "It has been a very dry spring. I have to water it every day. . . . We may have to replant the whole thing!" What is "it," you may ask—not a lawn or a window box but a sod roof.  There was a time, early this century, when sod roofs were the roof of choice in rural Alaska. And while they are less common today, people still use them in the bush for the same reasons: they provide reasonable insulation for the cost, are quick to build, and the necessary materials are always close at hand. For more urban settings like the visitor center in North Pole, the reason is different—they look cool. From the name, you might expect a sod roof to look like a well-groomed lawn, but in Alaska that's rarely the case. Occasionally people will plant wildflowers or several varieties of grass, but often the sod roof is simply left to germinate on its own. The result is a roof that looks like the land nearby, be it tundra, taiga forest, or mossy meadow, with an occasional birch, cottonwood, or spruce tree sprouting as a bonus.

◄ and ◄ ◄ The friendly folks at the North Pole Visitors Center greet motorists with a welcome sign and a dose of warm weather.

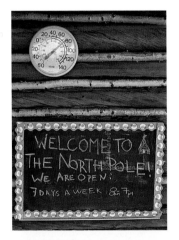

▲ Santa Claus House in North Pole.

ROBERTA'S ROADHOUSE

When Roberta Koppenberg came to Alaska from California, it wasn't long before she decided to stay. So when she heard that someone was selling an entire townsite for $20,000, she jumped at the opportunity. Of course, by 1974 the once-bustling gold town of Kantishna, established in 1905, wasn't much to look at: a tiny mining district recorder's office and a two-story roadhouse, both abandoned. Like Alaska gold rushes elsewhere, the Kantishna rush quickly brought thousands to the rolling hills forty miles north of

▲ The original log roadhouse in Kantishna provided food and lodging to local miners and travelers for many years.
▶ Roberta Koppenberg needed ten years to go from canvas tents and a plywood shack to the log Kantishna Roadhouse.

Mount McKinley, and nearly as quickly left just a handful behind. In 1983 Roberta offered to provide food and lodging for a mineral survey crew assaying claims in the area, and she set up twelve canvas wall tents and a thirty-by-forty-foot plywood cookhouse. "That's how the idea of the roadhouse was reborn," said Roberta, though she admits she had no idea how much work it would take to go from wall tents to the Kantishna Roadhouse she eventually sold in 1995. Over the next several years, five additions were made to the original cookhouse, an electric generator and water system were installed, and log cabins complete with indoor plumbing replaced the wall tents. Finally, in 1992, just before the roadhouse closed for the winter, Roberta decided to take the plunge and replace the old cookhouse with a real lodge. Her husband Sam was the architect and engineer, and her brother-in-law Jerome was the logsmith. "We prefabbed the entire building in an aircraft hanger in Fairbanks over the winter," Roberta said. "The hanger was fifty-two by fifty-two, and the building was forty-eight by fifty-two. We did the building in two sections, took it all apart and trucked it into Kantishna on May 21. We opened for business one week late on June 15." "We gambled everything to build that building," Roberta said, "but it was worth it."

▲ An inviting destination at the end of the day..
▼ Visitors admire the interior of the new lodge.

MOOSE RACK MADNESS

▲ Moose racks are to log cabins as hood ornaments are to old cars.
▶ No log cabin is complete without a set of moose antlers.

For thousands of years, Man has succumbed to the urge to create ornamentation. We have painted pictures in our caves, mounted gargoyles on our cathedrals, added gingerbread to our houses, and displayed millions of plastic gnomes, penguins, ducks, and pink flamingos on our lawns. ☰ People in Alaska are not immune to this primal obsession. We have had our share of plastic lawn animals. But we also have our own peculiarly Alaskan form of ornamentation: the moose rack. ☰ Now it's true that moose racks aren't as fanciful as gargoyles, or as tacky as plastic birds, but nail a moose rack to a log cabin and you have something

that goes together like a 1950s American car and a hood ornament. And when it comes to value, nothing can beat the moose rack. I know you can pick up a pink plastic bird for as little as a dollar at a good garage sale, but thanks to Mother Nature you can get a moose rack free of charge; bulls shed their antlers yearly. 🏠 You can't beat a deal like that.

▲ Think of moose racks as Alaska's answer to pink flamingoes.
◄ Luckily, moose don't have to sacrifice their lives to keep up with demand; bulls shed their antlers yearly.

FROM SOAPY SMITH TO SAUSAGES

▲ and ▶ ▲ This cabin may have been home to a thief and con man named "Skagway Jim" in the early 1900s.
▶ Annegret Wilder greets customers at her Alaskaland Restaurant in Fairbanks.

According to local historians, the Fairbanks cabin that is home to Annegret Wilder's German restaurant, called the Sausage Stop, was once home to a bad boy named Skagway Jim. Apparently Jim was a one-time member of Soapy Smith's gang of thieves, thugs, and con men who ran Skagway from 1897 until Soapy was killed in a shoot-out in 1898. ⌂ After Soapy's death, gang members scattered across Alaska, with Jim landing in Fairbanks, where he remained until his death several years later from an old gunshot wound. ⌂ Being a bit of a historian, Annegret studied her cabin's history. "I read all about Skagway and the

Klondike Gold Rush before I opened the restaurant in 1994," Annegret told me. Coming from Germany she had always found Alaska's history fascinating, but there is one point that she finds rather curious: Alaska history and architecture is all so . . . well, new. In Europe architecture isn't old unless its age is measured in centuries; in Alaska old is measured in decades. "My hometown in Germany was founded by Charlemagne in 800 A.D." Annegret said to me across the counter of her Alaskaland restaurant. "Now that's old!"

▲ Visitors sit a spell with an Alaska stuffed moose on the boardwalk at Alaskaland in Fairbanks.
◄ Annegret's hometown in Germany was founded more than 1,000 years ago, yet by Alaska standards these early-twentieth-century cabins across from her restaurant are old.

A PLACE OUT OF TIME

At the end of the nineteenth century, towns with names like Bergman, Peavy, Union City, Seaforth, Jimtown, and Arctic City sprang up on creeks surrounding the upper Koyukuk River. Most were little more than clearings in the woods and are long gone. But Wiseman, located eighty miles north of the Arctic Circle, survived—though just barely.

 Jan and Troy Thacker purchased the Wiseman Trading Company in 1995. The original trading post was built in nearby Coldfoot in 1910 and moved by river on a big raft to Wiseman in 1912, when the gold near Coldfoot began to peter out. After the original building burned down in 1927, the trading post was relocated into its present building, an old warehouse. Today Wiseman has no school, no post office, one telephone, and one

▲ The Wiseman Trading Company is the largest building in Wiseman.
▶ Jan Thacker and her husband, Troy, own the historic trading post, which dates back to 1910.

store: the Wiseman Trading Company ☖ "There's a real lure to living up here," Jan told me. "People live in these old cabins and sit on antique chairs and use turn-of-the-century china. In other places all that stuff would be in a museum. But here it's being used. People are living with it." ☖ In 1933 Wiseman was described as a place that is "two hundred miles beyond the edge of the twentieth century." Civilization may have moved a lot closer to Wiseman over the years, but when you are there you feel that the town is still over the edge.

▲ The interior hasn't changed much since the store opened in this building in 1927.
◄ Anywhere else, the Wiseman Trading Company would be a museum.

JACK AND JANE'S TRAIN

▲ Jack Seemann restored an eight-and-a-half-foot long steam locomotive on his homestead near Palmer.
▶ After Jack set seventy-five feet of track, a log train depot came next.

Jack Seemann has always loved trains. "When I was a kid I could hear the train whistle day and night," Jack told me. Jack also loves to see old things put to use. "I'm not much for museums. They put things behind glass and you can't touch them anymore." So it may have been inevitable that in 1992 Jack and his wife, Jane, bought a train of their own: a twelve-gauge (meaning the tracks are twelve inches apart) miniature train from an old timer in Florida. 🚊 From there things just seemed to snowball. "If you own a train you just have to have a depot," Jack said. So after restoring the eight-and-a-half-foot long steam engine to working condition and laying seventy-five feet of track on their Palmer

homestead, Jack and Jane started construction of a full-size log depot. It took nearly two years to complete. "It was my second attempt at using a dovetail notch. After I was finished, Jane had to cover up my mistakes," Jack confessed, showing me where Jane had neatly applied strips of Styrofoam® between the log rounds. 🏛 Even then Jack and Jane weren't done. "You can't have a train depot without people," Jack explained. So Jane made costumes, stuffed them with straw, and added masks. Now Barbara Bush sells tickets; George Bush is a conductor; Abraham Lincoln waits for a train; inside the station, Ross Perot and Jesse Jackson play cards. 🏛 And while all the characters are political, Jane swears it wasn't intentional. "It's just that after Halloween they were the only ones I could get cheap."

▲ After Jack built the depot, his wife, Jane, created historic figures to fill it.
◄ Jack and Jane Seemann put a leg up at the train depot saloon.

55

LOGGIN' A LITTLE RADIO TIME

At 180 feet, the log home of radio station KJNP (King Jesus in North Pole) is the longest log building in Alaska. It may be the largest log cabin in Alaska too, but nobody knows for sure.  Many years ago Don Nelson, an itinerant missionary from Minnesota, established the Evangelistic Alaska Missionary Fellowship on fifty-seven acres near North Pole. To spread the gospel across Alaska and beyond, Nelson started a

▲ KJNP broadcasts an Evangelical message to thousands of listeners across the north.

▶ At 180 feet, this is believed to be the longest and perhaps largest log building in Alaska.

ten-thousand-watt AM radio station in 1967 that was boosted to fifty thousand watts in 1970. Broadcasts are made in three Native languages, as well as English and Russian, and are heard via medium wave in Finland, Sweden, Norway, Russia, France, Germany, and Japan. Nelson added an FM station in 1977 and a TV station in 1981. And as the broadcasting mission expanded, the log cabin expanded right along with it.

▲ A colorful wreath brightens the exterior of the log cabin.
◀ Broadcasts are made in five languages to eight countries.

LARRY'S LIFELONG DREAM

▲ A greenhouse is a necessary part of any self-sufficient lifestyle.
▶ After several careers, Larry Earl fulfilled a dream when he moved to Tok and built a log cabin.

Larry Earl dreamed of living in a log cabin in Alaska since he was a boy watching *Sergeant Preston of the Yukon* on TV. "I would read my dad's *Outdoor Life* back in the '50s. Reading all the fishing stories and hunting stories and stories about wilderness was very appealing to me." 🏠 But there were lots of other things to do and, Larry thought, lots of time to do them. Finally, in 1996, after a career in the Navy and another as a travel writer, Larry decided the time had come to make his dream a reality. 🏠 "All my family and friends have shared in this adventure. People gave me candles, windows, doors, lighting fixtures, cast iron skillets. Everything. It took people about a year to gather it all together." 🏠 In May 1997 Larry brought "the stuff" to Tok from Spokane in a seventeen-foot rental truck. His brother-in-law Bud and friend Gary came along to share a bit of the dream.

◄ Larry sits back and appreciates his handiwork just before winter hits the northland.
◄▼ Nearly everything in Larry's cabin was donated by friends in Washington State.

Gary put in the long drive on the road to the cabin and Bud helped with the logs. 🏠 Larry admitted that once he arrived in Tok he had a real sense of urgency to complete the cabin and settle in before winter. "If I were here by myself I would have worked twenty-hour days. But with Gary and Bud here we ate dinners, we worked shorter days, we rested, we read. I sometimes got frustrated that I didn't have time to finish. But they didn't know that. I didn't want them to know that."

LOFTY LIVING

While a log cabin in Whitehorse, Yukon Territory, usually wouldn't appear in a book on Alaska's log buildings, in this case I just couldn't help myself. I've been fascinated with the log cabin "skyscraper" since I first visited Whitehorse in 1975. The original three-story building, completed in 1947 to ease a severe housing shortage, was raised an additional story in the early 1970s. Each floor is an identical sixteen-by-sixteen-foot studio apartment, complete with bathroom, kitchen, and electric heat. "I really enjoy living here," Lorene Robertson, the long-time "penthouse" resident, told me in a phone conversation. "I am fascinated with historical buildings. . . . I have a cabin out of town, but this is my urban retreat." Living in a tourist attraction in downtown Whitehorse does have its problems. "It lacks a certain element of privacy," Lorene admitted. And when the wind blows, which it does fairly often, the building sways "very noticeably." In fact, Lorene said, "When anybody walks on any of the floors I can feel it." She believes that someday the building will be taken over by the city. "Eventually it will be considered unsafe." Maybe, but until then Lorene is going to enjoy every day in her log penthouse apartment.

▲ Built in 1947, this three-story log cabin "skyscraper" is one of a kind.
▶ Lorene Robertson, who lives on the top floor, calls her penthouse home an "urban retreat."

LITTLE COFFEE CABIN

Michelle Rogers and Gerald Witmer weren't prepared for all the attention their Little Coffee Cabin has received since they purchased it in December 1996. "Tourists come by all the time and take pictures," Michelle told me. "Sometimes they get coffee, sometimes not. We put a chocolate-covered espresso bean on the coffee lid 'cause it looks like a moose turd. People get a kick out of it."

"We make a big effort to make the place look nice in the summer. We put out window boxes full of flowers." In fact, their window boxes were awarded third prize in a national contest held by a seed company. But the flowers caused a bit of confusion. "Before we put up the espresso sign, someone thought we sold flowers," Michelle said.

▲ Winter or summer, the Little Coffee Cabin serves up espresso to the locals.
▶ Some visitors mistake the espresso cabin for a cocktail lounge.
▶▲ Michelle Rogers and Gerald Witmer put chocolate-covered espresso beans on the coffee lids because they resemble moose droppings.

Another confusion was caused by their location next to Carpentier's Lounge. "In the winter, when the place was all lit up next to the sign that said 'Carpentier's Lounge — Darts and Pool,' somebody stopped by to see how we fit all that stuff into such a small space," Michelle told me. "Boy, was he surprised to see we just made coffee."

AP-PEELING PLACE TO LIVE

In 1977 Donna Blasor Bernhardt and her husband, Dick, pulled up stakes in Anchorage, moved to Tok with their two small children, and invested every dime they had in a piece of property and a pile of logs. "Our dream was to live in a log cabin," Donna said as we sat in the living room of her log home.  "I peeled nearly all of the logs and Dick worked them," Donna said. "I really got the taste of log sap in my mouth. Each log was different, unique really . . . I felt like a sculptor. Some of the knots are really cool. There is one that has a perfect beaver face; another is a perfect profile of a mallard. We would deliberately turn the logs so we could have our own art collection on the walls.

▲ Old kerosene lamps and hanging planters decorate the porch.
▶ Donna Blasor Bernhardt peeled the logs by hand for this cabin that she and her husband, Dick Bernhardt, built together.

▲ Donna's bedroom under a red-curtained skylight.
◀ Donna's daughter Katherine and granddaughter Brianne play on the floor of the cabin during a visit to Tok.

🏠 "Our history and the trees' histories have merged," Donna continued. "I know this sounds hokey, but a lot of the love that went into the preparation of the logs has come back to us. I can sit here and remember each log and remember what we did to get it there. It's full of memories, full of history . . . living history." 🏠 Some of that history has included the death of her husband and the growth of her children into adulthood, yet Donna's feelings for the cabin have never changed. "When I walk in here, I feel that the cabin is embracing me. I love my cabin. I can't imagine living in any other place."

LAST WORD

Except for another book on outhouses, log cabins seemed the natural choice for my second book. Though perhaps not as obviously quirky as some of the subjects of my first book, *Outhouses of Alaska*, log cabins and their owners are quintessentially Alaska. 🏠 Once decided, I had no trouble finding material. If anything, I had trouble editing the possibilities down to the 31 stories contained in these pages. Often I would set off to photograph one building I had read about, only to stumble on another one I found far more interesting. Or, in the course of my travels, I would meet somebody who had a friend who knew somebody who once lived near a cabin they thought might interest me. 🏠 As with all great adventures, I never knew exactly where I was headed, whom I might meet, or what I might learn. This project may be finished but my continuing search to find the real Alaska goes on.

► Author-photographer Harry M. Walker on top of the situation at a log dog kennel along the Glenn Highway.